WOWEE ZOWEE

a flight of imagination

Welcome to Wowee Zowee the airline of imagination. Today we will be visiting some weird worlds and peculiar planets. We'll need you to have your pencils and pens at the ready so that we can make the most of the adventures to come!

WOWEE P.P. POSTOFFICE 22.6.2021 ZOWEE

T0016127

ARE YOU READY?

Before we board the plane, let's check that we've packed everything we need.

Make sure you've got a good book to read ...

Oh no! My buddy is missing!

No worries, I'm right here!

Is your favourite teddy coming with you? Draw him here

... You'll definitely need some more coloured pencils!

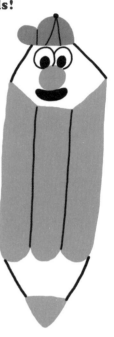

Don't forget to bring snacks!

And you'll need some spare pants too!

CATWICK AIRPORT

DEPARTURE

CHECK IN →

Welcome to Catwick Airport. The Wowee Zowee plane departs from gate number 52. Thank you and enjoy your trip!

MILKBAR *Biscuits*

NICE

Draw some more cats please!

51-93 →

MICE

MICE MICE

MICE MICE MICE

FI SH

← 1-50

GLATSCH

WHISKER

CAT TODAY

SUG AR

SK8 CAT

← 61-75

51-60 →

Quick!
I need the
loo!

Oh dear, there's
a hole in my bag!
I've lost 25 biscuits.
Can you help me
find them?

TOILET

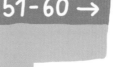

MICE
TO MEAT
YOU

← 51-75

76-93 →

52

You made it just in time!
Draw the queue of people
ready to board.

VECTOLAND

Our first stop is

**Geometry is always on trend in Vectoland.
Look at all the strange shapes!**

Excuse me,
Mr Triangle,
have you seen
Half Moon Cat
anywhere?

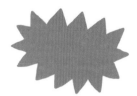

Meow

Hi Mr Squarepants, I think Half Moon Cat is hiding in the trees.

Fill the page with some of your own vector creatures

VECTOSHOP

Welcome to Vectoshop. Can you help stock our shelves with some cool geometric products? Our customers like them to be super wacky!

FRUITNVEG MEGABURB

The centre of Megaburb is already busy, but at rush hour it gets even busier. Let's make it super crowded!

Hi Kiko, I'll meet you at Bean Burger Barn.

Where is Yoshi?

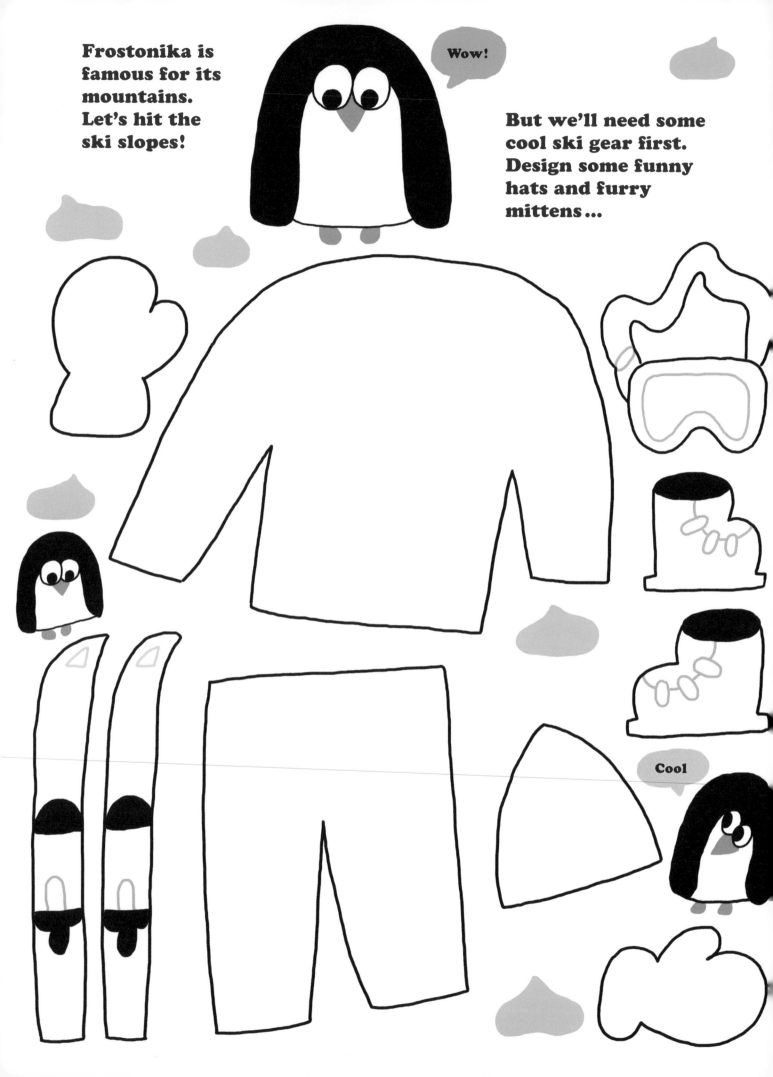

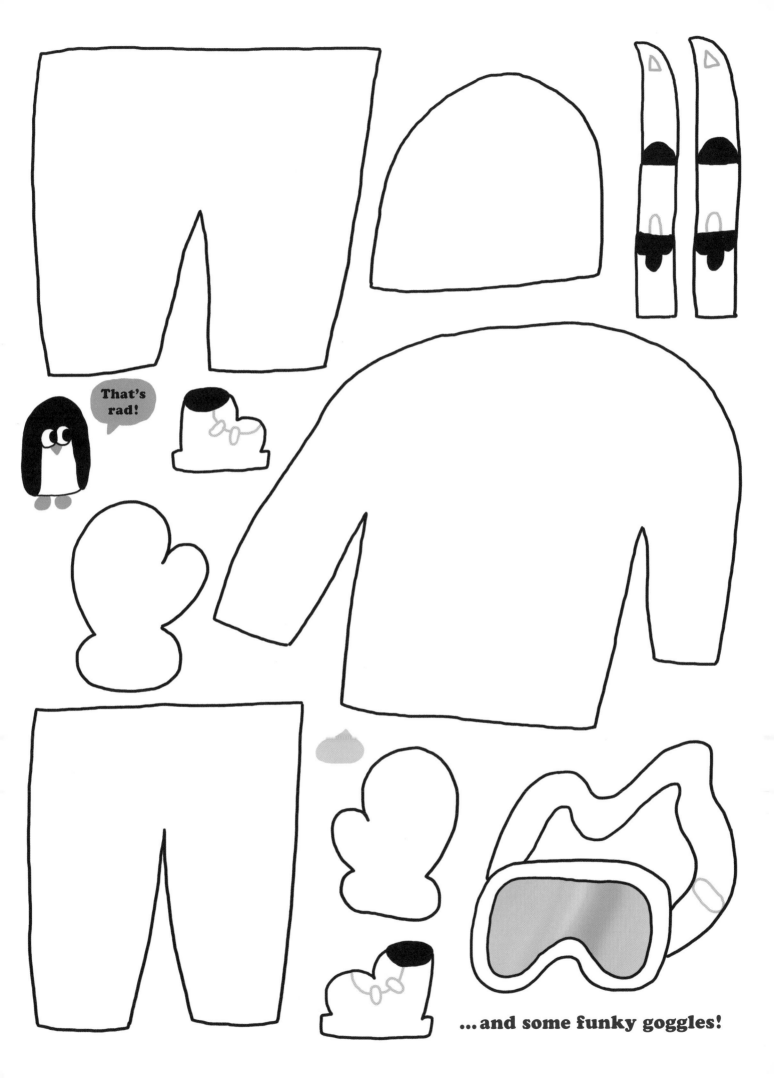

Put on some suncream and grab a deckchair. Let's catch some rays!

BEACHBAR

DRINKS

SNACKS

Colour in the island with some bright, tropical colours.

BEACHBAR

Time for a snack. Will you mix us some refreshing drinks? Give them funny names.

Don't forget the peanuts!

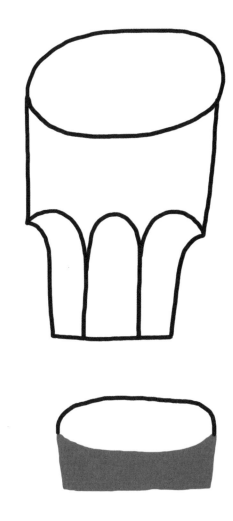

Menu

There are some yummy local specials on the menu. What are they?

Uh oh...
Mount Pipapo is about to erupt... we'd better get out of here!

Phew! We made it back onto the plane in the nick of time. But after all that eating and drinking, we need the toilet. Oh sugar, there is already a long queue! Draw yourself into the shoes below.

Colour
by numbers:
1 is blue
2 is green
3 is lovely pink
4 is yellow
5 is airplane grey
6 is red
7 is yuck brown

Our next stop is... OLDE-FOREST

Olde-Forest is home to many woodland creatures and seven cheeky dwarves. Poopsie and Whoopsie are already hard at work. Can you draw the other dwarves?

There's a nasty, grumpy litterbug hiding on the page. Can you spot him?

Oh no! Squirrel's tail is missing. Can you help me fix it?

This forest should be full of trees and mushrooms like in ancient times.

Have some water

Oh nuts! The litterbug has left 23 pieces of rubbish around the forest! Can you pick them all up?

Thanks for helping to tidy up. Now it's time to hop back on board. Our next stop will be Crystal Castles.

CRYSTAL CASTLES

Error score:

In Crystal Castles everything is reflected perfectly. Two identical kings rule over the reflections from two identical palaces.

But wait! Mirage Patrol has found 18 faults with the reflections today. Can you help spot the differences?

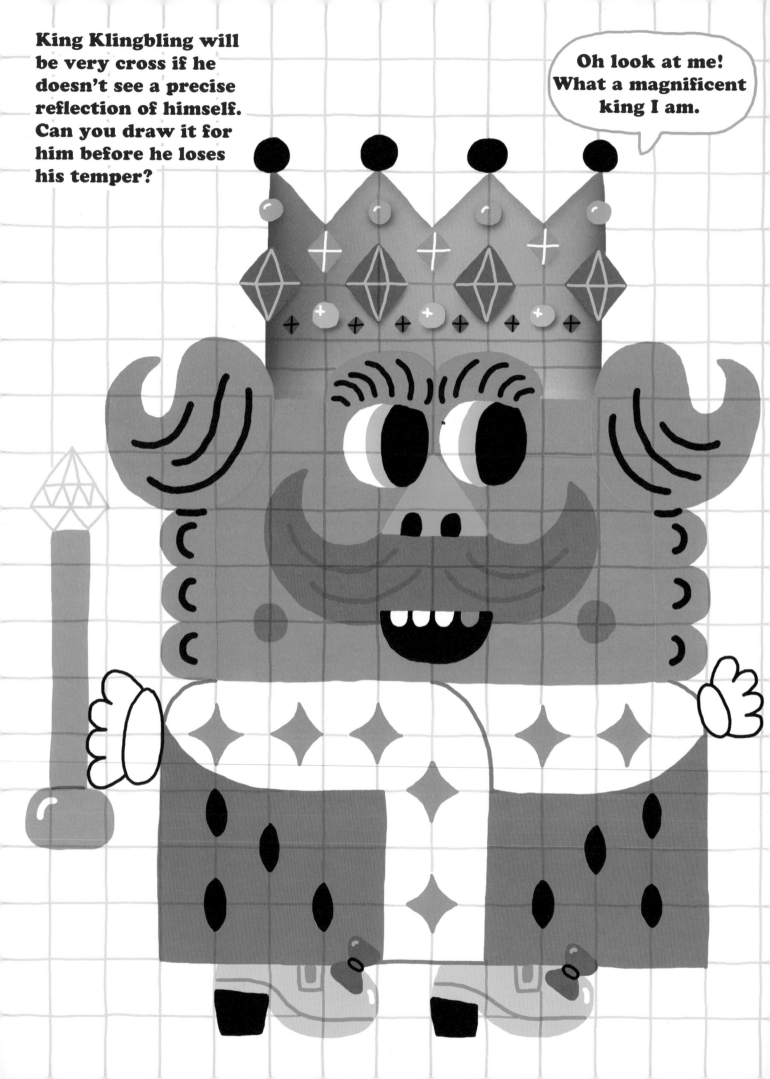

My face is looking even more handsome than usual today!

Have you drawn a perfect copy of King Klingbling? Are you sure? Then hop back on board. Time to head back to Catwick Airport.

They are all very tired.
Draw some beds for our
new friends to sleep in.

Well that was an epic adventure.
We're sure we'll have some
wild dreams tonight!

Thank you for flying with Wowee Zowee, the airline of imagination. Come back soon!